Travel Through the British Isles

Lynn Huggins-Cooper
QEB Publishing

First published in the United States by
QEB Publishing, Inc.
23062 La Cadena Drive
Laguna Hills, CA 92653

www.qeb-publishing.com

Library of Congress Control Number: 2007000946

ISBN 978 1 59566 360 3

Written by: Lynn Huggins-Cooper
Designed by: Manishi Varshney (Q2A Media)
Editor: Honor Head
Picture Researcher: Sujatha Menon (Q2A Media)

Publisher Steve Evans
Creative Director Zeta Davies
Senior Editor Hannah Ray

Printed and bound in China

Picture credits

Key: t = top, b = bottom, m = middle,
l = left, r = right, FC = front cover

Science Photo Library/ Photolibrary: 4 (background), 9t, 18b, Carsten Reisinger/ **Shutterstock:**
4t, 4br, Dimitrios Kaisaris/ **Shutterstock:** 4m, Dkessaris | **Dreamstime.com:** 4bl, Matthew Dixon/
Istockphoto: 6b, Gareth McCormack/ **Lonely Planet Images:** 7tl, 7tr, Eoin Clarke/ **Lonely Planet
Images:** 7b, Bethune Carmichae/ **Lonely Planet Images:** 8, Nina Pope: 9b, Manfred Gottschalk/
Lonely Planet Images: 10b, Pearl Bucknall/ **PhotolibraryWales.com:** 11t, Neil Setchfield / **Lonely
Planet Images:** 11b, PAUL GLENDELL / **Still Pictures:** 12t, **Robert Harding Picture Library
Ltd/ Photolibrary:** 12b, Nicholas Reuss/ **Lonely Planet Images:** 13m, Rachael: 14t, Thomas Bendy/
Istockphoto: 14b, **Index Stock Imagery/ Photolibrary:** 15t, Nathan Middleton/ **Fotolibra:** 16t,
Patrick Ward/**CORBIS:** 16b, **Jtb Photo Communications Inc/ Photolibrary:** 17t, Tim Page/**CORBIS:**
19t, **Huw Jones, HLJ Photography:** 19b, Glenn Miles/ **Fotolibra:** 20b, Jon Davison/ **Lonely Planet
Images:** 21t, Dale O'Dell / **Alamy:** 21b, **David Robertson Photography, photographersdirect.
com:** 23t, Kit Houghton/**CORBIS:** 23b, Patrick Horton/ **Lonely Planet Images:** 24b, Graeme
Cornwallis/ **Lonely Planet Images:** 25t, Christer Fredriksson/ **Lonely Planet Images:** 25b, **Oxford
Scientific Films/ Photolibrary:** 26b, Linda Wright/ **Fotolibra:** 27t, Paul Glendell / **Alamy:** 27b.

Words in **bold** can be found in the glossary on page 31.

Contents

Where in the world are the British Isles?.........5

What are the British Isles like? 6

Food and drink 8

Getting around...10

The coast..12

Capital cities 14

Heritage and history....................................16

Farming in the British Isles 18

Myths and legends of the British Isles 20

Festivals and holidays 22

Climate 24

Conservation and the environment 26

Activity ideas 28

Glossary 31

Index...32

Atlantic
Ocean

Shetland Islands

Orkney Islands

Wick

SCOTLAND

Outer Hebrides

Skye

Aberdeen

Inner
Hebrides

NORTHERN IRELAND

Edinburgh

Farne Islands

North Sea

Isles of Arran

Derry

Newcastle

Sligo

Belfast

York

Isle of Man

Hull

Galway

Irish Sea

Liverpool

Dublin

Anglesey

ENGLAND

Aran Islands

Llandudno

Limerick

Birmingham

Kerry

Cambridge

Cork

Oxford

London

REPUBLIC
OF IRELAND

Cardiff

Bath

WALES

Dover

Brighton

Lands End

Isle of Wight

Plymouth

English Channel

Isles of Scilly

Where in the world are the British Isles?

The British Isles is a group of islands in northwest Europe. It includes the large islands of Great Britain (made up of Wales, England, and Scotland) and Ireland (made up of Northern Ireland and the Republic of Ireland —also known as Eire). There are also many smaller surrounding islands, such as the Isle of Man, the Inner and Outer Hebrides, the Isles of Scilly, the Channel Islands, the Isle of Wight, the Farne Islands, the Isles of Arran, Anglesey, and the Orkneys.

Though it does not cover a particularly large area, as you travel through the British Isles, you will experience an exciting mix of different landscapes, climates, peoples, foods, and traditions.

Did you know?

OFFICIAL NAME: The British Isles

LOCATION: Western Europe

SURROUNDING SEAS AND OCEANS: Atlantic Ocean, English Channel, North Sea, Irish Sea

CAPITAL CITIES: London (England); Cardiff (Wales); Edinburgh (Scotland); Belfast (Northern Ireland); Dublin (Republic of Ireland)

AREA: 121,674 sq. mi. (315,134 sq. km)

POPULATION: 63,000,000

LIFE EXPECTANCY: Male: 76 years Female: 81 years

RELIGION: Mainly Christian (72%)

LANGUAGES: English, Welsh, Gaelic

CLIMATE: **temperate**

HIGHEST MOUNTAIN: Scafell Pike (England, 3,209 ft./978 m); Carrantouhill (Republic of Ireland, 3,415 ft./1,041 m); Slieve Donard (Northern Ireland, 2,789 ft./850 m); Ben Nevis (Scotland, 4,409 ft./1,344 m); Snowdon (Wales, 3,560 ft./1,085 m)

MAJOR RIVERS: Severn (England, 217 mi./350 km long); Shannon (Republic of Ireland, 240 mi./386 km long); Bann (Northern Ireland, 80 mi./129 km); Tay (Scotland, 120 mi./193 km); Towy (Wales, 64 mi./103 km)

CURRENCY: Pound Sterling; Euro

What are the British Isles like?

Traveling through the British Isles you will see a mixture of old and new. The British Isles has a long history, so there are many ancient monuments and historic buildings to visit. Scattered throughout the countryside, you will see traditional, old villages with **thatched** cottages and **beamed** buildings. However, there are also many large, lively cities to visit, too, with plenty of exciting things to see and do.

Caernarfon Castle in Wales is one of the many castles you can visit in the British Isles.

Tourists love to visit Tower Bridge, built over the River Thames in London, in 1894.

The British Isles has many beautiful bays and beaches. This lovely, sandy beach is at Keem Strand in County Mayo, in the Republic of Ireland.

Landscapes

There are many different types of landscapes in the British Isles. You can trek across **moorland** in Devon, in southwest England, or go hill walking in the Lake District in northern England. You can visit a variety of coastal habitats, from craggy cliffs and rockpools to beautiful beaches in the west of Ireland. There is also much wonderful woodland to enjoy—such as the Caledonian Forest in Scotland.

Multicultural Britain

Since the 1950s, the British Isles has become a **multicultural** society. Many people have **emigrated** to the British Isles to live and work. As you travel through the towns and cities of the British Isles, you will see the ways that people from all over the world have enriched the British Isles with their culture and customs.

More than 6,000 islands make up the British Isles.

Climate

The British Isles has many different climates, from the **subtropical** warmth of the Isles of Scilly in the path of the **Gulf Stream**, to the colder temperatures of the beautiful Orkney Islands, off the coast of Scotland.

Hiking is popular and there are many hills to explore, such as the Aonach Eagach near Glencoe, in Scotland.

Food and drink

As well as a full English breakfast, you can also get a full Scottish, a full Welsh, and a full Irish breakfast, which all include slightly different foods.

Many people in the British Isles buy and cook food from big supermarkets. Here, you will see food that has been flown in from all around the world, but there are still many small shops and restaurants which sell local specialties.

Regional dishes

In Wales, you might see laver bread or "bara lawr" on menus. This bread is made from seaweed collected at low tide and boiled to make a type of jelly. The jelly is mixed with oats and lots of seasoning and then made into **patties** and fried. If you ask for bread rolls in a bakery in Newcastle, you may get stottie cakes. These aren't actually cakes but thick, large, flat bread rolls. If you went to Scotland, you might try haggis. This is meat, spices, and oatmeal stuffed into a case, like a sausage. It is usually served with neeps and tatties—mashed swede and potatoes.

Haggis is a savory dish traditionally made from sheep's "pluck"— the heart, liver, and lungs. Today, vegetarian haggis is also available.

Big breakfast

If you order a full English breakfast in a café, you would receive a plate loaded with some or all of the following: bacon, eggs, sausages, fried bread, fried tomatoes, mushrooms, **bubble and squeak**, **black pudding**, and baked beans.

Fish and chips

At the seashore, you might like some fish and chips. This is fish fried in batter and served with thick potato chips. Fish and chips can be bought in most towns in the British Isles—but many people think they taste best eaten on a windy beach!

Last week, I went to visit Grandpa in Devon. We went for a long walk along the beach and explored the rockpools. Grandpa said that the fresh air had given him an appetite, so we went to a tea shop and had a Devon cream tea. I had two scones, which are small, plain cakes. They are served with a little dish of strawberry jelly and a little dish of **clotted cream**. You cut the scones in half and fill them with jam and cream—yum!

Ben

Fish and chips have been popular all over the British Isles since Victorian times. Salt and vinegar is usually added.

Getting around

As in many other countries, lots of people in the British Isles travel by car. There are many big highways that make traveling from place to place easy, but traffic can be heavy, especially around large cities. You can also travel around the British Isles using trains, coaches, and buses. Many cities have underground railways, too, such as the London Underground and the Tyneside Metro system.

Planes and boats

There are many small **regional** airports as well as larger, well-known ones, such as Heathrow in London. You can take both internal flights from one area of the British Isles to another, or fly abroad. A ferry can take you to Ireland and to many of the smaller islands of the British Isles, such as the Isle of Wight. **Hovercrafts** and **hydrofoils** also hop backward and forward between the British Isles and mainland Europe.

The Snowdon Mountain Railway was built in 1896.

You can travel from the British Isles to mainland Europe on a ferry.

P&O Stena

Take the train

You can travel all over the British Isles by train, which is a great way to see the scenery. There are even a few old steam trains that run for tourists, such as the Snowdon Mountain Railway in Wales. The Channel Tunnel, built under the English Channel, links the British Isles with France and Belgium.

Some of the riverboats on the River Thames, in London, have restaurants. Tourists can enjoy a meal as they cruise along.

I just got back from my school trip to London. We went to loads of museums. The London Underground train system is amazing. It's incredible to think you can travel all over London through tunnels beneath the ground! We took a trip down the Thames on a riverboat. A guide told us about all the things you could see. My favorite was the view of the Tower of London, the old palace and prison owned for centuries by the kings and queens of England. The guide told us spooky stories about headless queens, prisoners, and ghosts!
Love,
Eleanor

The coast

As you travel around the coastline of the British Isles, you will see many different types of landscapes and animals, as well as many shore towns and cities.

Coastal creatures

The coastline of Scotland is very rugged and is made up of beautiful beaches and spectacular, rocky cliffs. Many different types of animals live around the Scottish coast. You can see countless seabirds, both common and gray seals, and other sea creatures, such as whales, porpoises, dolphins, and basking sharks.

Many shore towns and cities have piers. Brighton pier, in the southeast of England, was built in Victorian times and is still in use today.

PALACE PIER

TO TAKE AWAY
FISH & CHIPS   TEA
                COFFEE

Wonderful Wales

Puffins are found in parts of the British Isles, such as the Farne Islands off the coast of Northumbria.

If you visit the Gower Peninsula in Wales, you will find many beautiful beaches and coves. There are limestone cliffs to walk along and stretches of sandy beach to play on. In some places, such as Llangennith Sands, you can even go surfing.

he tiny Channel Island of Herm has a beach made of shells that were carried there by the Gulf Stream.

Brighton is great! I went with my family last weekend. We went on the pier and I won a cuddly dolphin on the tin-can alley game. Afterward, we had hot doughnuts, fresh from the pan. They were great, but I got covered in sugar. I went on a ride which swung out over the ocean and was really scary! Then Mom said she wanted to go for a walk through The Lanes, some tiny, twisty streets with amazing shops. After lunch in a nice cafe, we went to the Royal Pavilion, which was very cool! It is an Indian-style palace that George, Prince Regent (who became King George IV of England in 1820), had remodeled so he had somewhere to stay when he came to visit the city.
Love, Beth

At Rhossili Bay, on the Gower Peninsula in Wales, huge waves roar in from the Atlantic Ocean, making the beaches great for surfers!

Capital cities

Gorgeous murals and gold leaf decorate many walls inside the magnificent Cardiff Castle.

As you travel through the cities of the British Isles, you will see that each capital has its own style, from bustling London to elegant Dublin.

London

In London, it is easy for visitors to imagine they are on a film set, especially when they visit Buckingham Palace, where the Queen lives, or parliament at Whitehall. However, London is not just for tourists. Seven and a half million people live and work in this busy capital city.

The Swiss Re Tower in the financial district of London is known as "The Gherkin" because of its unusual shape.

Cardiff

The capital city of Wales is Cardiff (*Caerdydd* in Welsh). There is a lot to see and do. You can visit Cardiff Castle, which has the remains of a Roman settlement and a Norman castle. *Techniquest*, in the Cardiff Bay area, has a Science Discovery Center with 160 interactive exhibits and a planetarium.

Dublin

Dublin, or *Baile Átha Cliath* in Gaelic, is the capital of the Republic of Ireland. It has many historic buildings and wide, tree-lined streets. Dublin Castle stands on the site of a Viking fortress. A castle of some type has stood there ever since.

Edinburgh

There are many historic buildings, such as Edinburgh Castle and the shops on the Royal Mile in the capital city of Scotland (*Dùn Èideann* in Gaelic). It is well known for the Edinburgh Festival, held in August, when thousands of visitors flock to see a wide variety of dancers, musicians, and actors performing.

Belfast has wide roads and streets filled with many beautiful Victorian buildings.

Belfast

The capital of Northern Ireland is on the mouth of the River Lagan. The world's largest **dry dock** is in Belfast, and it is where the ship *Titanic* was built. The center of Belfast is for pedestrians only, so it is relaxing to wander around without worrying about traffic. There are many shops to explore, and Victorian architecture and sculptures to look at.

 YOU'VE GOT MAIL

Hi! We visited Cardiff Castle today— it looks like a medieval fairytale castle! We had a tour of the apartments and clock tower, and then went to a banquet in the undercroft—it's the place where the bodies of important people would be kept and buried after they died. There were people dressed up in medieval costumes singing as we ate. Tina x

Heritage and history

The British Isles has a long history, full of invaders and settlers. There are many castles and **fortifications** in the British Isles that tell the story of wars and battles fought against these invaders.

Picts

Hadrian's Wall in Northumbria is a 73 mi. (118 km) long wall built in Roman times to keep a fierce tribe called the **Picts** from invading the rest of England. The wall stretched from the west to the east coast.

Celts

Ireland has many sites where you can see remains left behind by the tribes who lived there from 2, 500 B.C.E. There are many stone circles and tombs. Some stone circles are places where ancient **Celts** used to worship their gods.

Hadrian, a Roman Emperor in 117 C.E., invaded Britain and gave orders to build the famous wall.

Dunstanburgh Castle is a 14th-century castle in Northumberland, England. It looks out over wild coastline.

Shakespeare's birthplace has displays that show how people lived in Elizabethan times, when Shakespeare was alive.

Walk with Shakespeare

If you go to Stratford-upon-Avon, in central England, you can visit many historic buildings, including the birthplace of the playwright William Shakespeare. This is a beautiful, old, beamed building—and it is incredible to think that you can walk in rooms where Shakespeare walked nearly 450 years ago. Shakespeare's plays are still performed in Stratford-upon-Avon's three theaters, and also in the Globe Theater, by the River Thames in London. The Globe Theater was rebuilt on the original site where many of Shakespeare's plays were first acted.

See, hear, and smell

Farther north, you can visit the city of York with its Viking remains. The Jorvik Viking Center tells the story of the Viking invasion and settlement in the British Isles. There is a "sight and sound" display to ride around—with stinky smells of the time, too!

Hadrian's Wall is one of my favorite places to visit. You can see it stretching away, far into the distance. You can try on some armor at a Roman museum called Vindolanda. There is a re-creation of a Roman banquet and guess what, they ate stuffed dormice!

Love, Iona

17

Farming in the British Isles

Orchards are found all over the British Isles. Apples are grown for eating, cooking, and making into cider, an alcoholic drink.

As you travel around the British Isles, you will see lots of open farmland. About three-quarters of the land in the British Isles is used for a mixture of **arable** and **livestock** farming.

Many working farms in the British Isles ha vacation cottages whe you can stay and eve help out on the farm

Sheep in the hills

Sheep are farmed all over the British Isles, even in wild, mountainous areas, such as the hill farms in Wales. Many farmers round up their sheep using trained Border Collie dogs.

Sheep are farmed for wool, sheepskin fleeces, meat, and milk.

Fruits and vegetables

Many different crops are grown in the British Isles, such as wheat, corn, and barley, as well as vegetables. There are also orchards full of apples and pears. A lot of soft fruit, such as strawberries and raspberries, are grown, and many farms have "pick your own" options, which means you pay a fee and then collect your own fruit, fresh from the fields.

Organic food

You can now buy a lot of organically grown food—that means that no chemicals have been used on the crops. Much of this food is sold at farmers' markets around the British Isles. Farmers and **smallholders** bring their goods to sell directly to the public at the markets.

YOU'VE GOT MAIL

I've been helping Mom with the harvest on our farm. I seem to have picked hundreds and hundreds of apples! We are taking all the apples to a farmers' market in Durham, in northern England. People come from all over to buy our apples because they're organic, and they're old English varieties such as "Ribstone Pippin" and "Knobby Russet" that you can't buy in the supermarkets any more.

Mom and I are taking the horsebox down to the National Fruit Collection at Brogdale, in Kent, next week —this is a special collection of fruit trees and bushes. In fact, it's the largest collection of varieties of fruit trees in the world. We plan to buy some new trees to make the orchard even bigger. We'll need the horsebox to bring them home.
Alex

Farmers bring all sorts of fresh fruit and vegetables to sell at the market.

Myths and legends of the British Isles

The British Isles has a fine storytelling tradition, full of tales of brave heroes and fierce monsters.

Busy giant

In Ireland, you'll hear tales of Celtic heroes such as the giant, Fionn Mac Cumhaill. The myth says that the Giant's Causeway in County Antrim, Northern Ireland, was made when Fionn decided to build a bridge across the sea between Ireland and Scotland. Another legend says he threw a clod of earth at a Scottish giant. The clod landed in the sea and became the Isle of Man.

Giant killer

Natural features all over the British Isles have inspired storytellers. St. Michael's Mount in Cornwall, southwest England, is a tiny island that can be reached by a causeway only at low tide. Set on a rocky, granite crag, it is said to be the place where a fearsome giant named Cormoran lived and terrorized the local people. Legend tells of a farmer's son named Jack, who is said to have lured Cormoran away from the Mount and trapped him in a huge pit. Jack the Giant Killer then traveled around the British Isles, killing other giants.

The Giant's Causeway is a stone structure made from volcanic rock.

King Arthur

If you travel to Somerset, you will hear about Glastonbury Tor (tor means "rocky hill"). It is said to be the sacred Isle of Avalon, where King Arthur was taken after he fought with the evil sorcerer, Mordred. King Arthur was the legendary king who gathered at the famous Round Table with his knights. The legend says Arthur still waits on Avalon for the day when Britain needs a hero.

The Tower of St. Michael at Glastonbury Tor.

Loch Ness is an amazing 23.5m (38 km) long and on average (2 km) wide. It is up to (225 m) deep.

Loch Ness monster

No visit to Scotland would be complete without a visit to **Loch** Ness to look for the monster which is said to live there. Some people even think the monster is a dinosaur, left over from prehistoric times. Many people claim to have seen the monster but no one has ever been able to prove that the monster really exists.

Some people think Nessie may be a stray seal—or even a dinosaur!

Festivals and holidays

The British Isles has many different festivals and fairs. As you travel from place to place, you can see traditions that have survived to the present day.

Bonfire Night

On November 5th, the British Isles is lit up with bonfires and fireworks. Bonfire Night remembers the discovery of a plan to blow up parliament by a man called Guy Fawkes in 1605. The plan was called The Gunpowder Plot. As you travel from town to town, you may see a "Guy" on many bonfires. The Guy is like a scarecrow and is burned on the fire.

In Lewes, in East Sussex in England, a great parade is held on Bonfire Night. Many people dress up in historical costumes.

Lewes has many Bonfire Societies who all take part in the celebrations on November 5th.

Hogmanay

In Scotland, Christmas is celebrated in much the same way as the rest of the British Isles. But it is at Hogmanay, which brings in the New Year on the night of 31st December, when the biggest celebrations take place, with street parties and lively processions.

Fireballs

Throughout the British Isles, amazing Fire Ceremonies take place that are linked with the **winter solstice**, or midwinter. At Stonehaven, on the northeast coast of Scotland, you can see giant fireballs being swung around on long metal poles.

Spectacular firework displays light up the sky at Hogmanay.

Boys ride their horses through a river at the Appleby Fair.

This weekend I went to Appleby Fair in Cumbria (in the north of England) with Grandpa. He's been coming since he was a little boy. We went all the way in Grandpa's vardo—an old-fashioned gypsy caravan. My horse Khola pulled the wagon all the way to Appleby. Grandpa said there's been a gypsy horse fair at Appleby since 1685. There were many people selling horses and having trotting races. There were riders "flashing" the ponies—galloping them down the lanes near the fair, so people could see them. It was a little scary! Down in the town, people were riding the horses across the river.
Ellie x

Climate

The British Isles has a temperate climate. This means it does not have extreme weather conditions. However, a temperate climate is often very changeable, so even in summer it can be sunny one day and rainy the next. Sensible visitors to the British Isles always carry an umbrella!

Seasons

The British Isles has very clear seasons. If you travel there in spring, it will be cool with showers and a little sunshine. Bulbs such as daffodils and tulips come into flower at this time. Summer can be hot, especially in areas such as the Isles of Scilly. Fall in the British Isles is beautiful, as the leaves change color from green to gold and red. Winter can be very cold.

People walk in the woods in the fall to see the changing leaves.

In the far north of the British Isles, snowfall can be deep during the winter.

Snowy weather

There are some differences in climate as you travel through the British Isles. The north of Scotland, for example, tends to get colder, longer winters than the south of England. Heavy, lasting snowfall is only likely in the northern parts of the British Isles, or on high ground such as in Snowdonia, in Wales.

Warm air

In general, the British climate is mild for its **latitude**. This is because of the Gulf Stream, a warm ocean current that starts out in the Gulf of Mexico and flows across the Atlantic ocean.

The temperature in the the British Isles can be as high as 86°F (30°C) in summer and below freezing in winter.

Summer vacations at the seashore in the British Isles are still popular.

Conservation and the environment

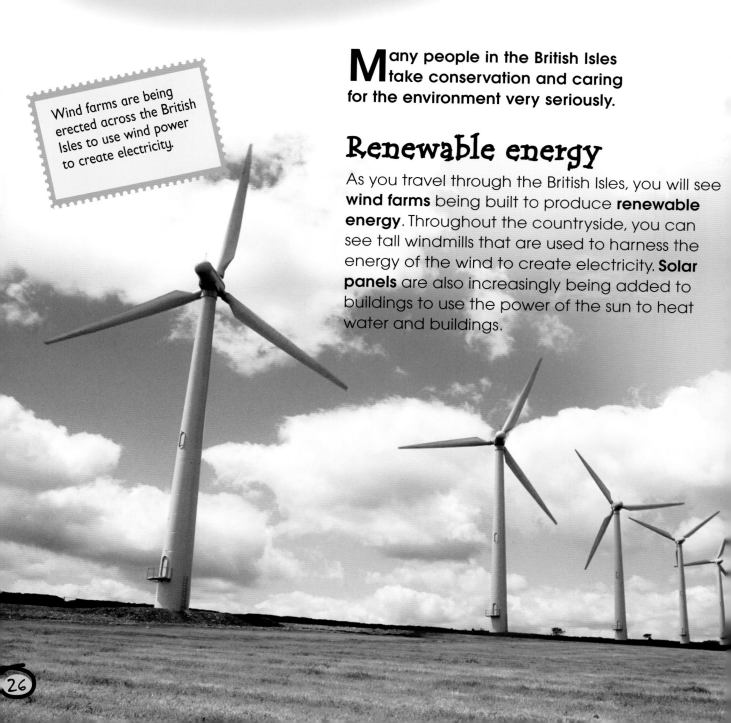

Wind farms are being erected across the British Isles to use wind power to create electricity.

Many people in the British Isles take conservation and caring for the environment very seriously.

Renewable energy

As you travel through the British Isles, you will see **wind farms** being built to produce **renewable energy**. Throughout the countryside, you can see tall windmills that are used to harness the energy of the wind to create electricity. **Solar panels** are also increasingly being added to buildings to use the power of the sun to heat water and buildings.

Recycling

The government is taking steps to greatly reduce the amount of waste sent to **landfill sites**, where it rots slowly and releases poisonous chemicals and **greenhouse gases** into the air. Many local councils collect plastic, paper, glass, and tin to recycle, and give householders free compost bins to collect kitchen waste to use in the garden.

Freecycle

All over the British Isles there are local **freecycle** groups. These groups encourage people to give away possessions they don't want to people who need them. If you have an item you no longer use, you add it to an e-mail list. If somebody wants your item, they reply and come and collect it. This saves the possessions from being taken to landfill sites, and helps the environment as well as other people.

I have joined the Conservation Club at school. This week we have been finding out about The Wildlife Trusts. Many plant and animal species in the British Isles, such as the Red Kite, are protected by law so that they do not become extinct. The Wildlife Trusts tell people how to help care for these animals and even how to build special habitats or places for creatures and plants to live, either in nature reserves or in their own gardens.
Ruby

On the weekend, my Cub Scout troop took part in a "clean beaches" campaign to collect litter left on the coast. Sadly, we found a lot. We are making posters for our Web site to show the dangers of pollution to sea life, as well as the effect litter has on tourism and the livelihoods of fishermen.
Mike

Activity ideas

1 Make a 3D map of the British Isles using papier mâché. Draw the rough shape on a sheet of cardstock, and add pieces of crumpled paper, glued firmly in place. Coat the model in PVA glue, and cover the whole model carefully with tissue paper. Push the paper carefully into all the inlets and coves you have created. Repeat this step until you have a smooth surface and leave to dry. Then paint and label your model.

2 Find a recipe for regional food from the British Isles —the Internet is a good source. With an adult, cook the food and eat a typical British meal. You could also buy some examples of regional foods and sample them, before reviewing them and displaying the reports of the "food critics."

NOTE FOR ADULTS: Please ensure that children do not suffer from any food allergies before making or eating any food.

3 Make a fact file about the Channel Tunnel—and then create a model. Make the tunnel by bending a sheet of thin cardstock into a tunnel shape and attaching it to a base—the side from a strong cardboard box will do. Paint the model with brown paint mixed with a little PVA glue for strength. Tear strips of blue tissue paper, crêpe paper, and cellophane in shades of blue and stick them to the base board, on either side of the tunnel—this will be the sea. You could even add clay sea creatures!

4 Using travel brochures, cut out pictures and make a collage to show the image of the British Isles given to tourists. What ideas and pictures do travel agents use to "sell" the British Isles as a tourist destination? Make a list of 10 words used in the brochures to persuade people to visit the British Isles.

5 Carry out research using the Internet, magazines, and newspapers to find out more about renewable energy in the British Isles. Use your information to debate with friends or classmates "for" and "against" renewable energy.

6 With an adult, visit a local farmers' market and see how far the food has traveled before you buy it. Compare these "food miles" with food bought at the supermarket.

7 Plan a trip around the British Isles. If you could pick ten places, where would you go? Why? How would you travel around?

8 Using a word-processing computer program, make a booklet showing the different types of coastal features that can be found around Britain. These should include cliffs, rocky beaches, and sand dunes —you will be amazed at how many you can find. Cut and paste photos from the Internet and place them with the text. Print your fact file.

9 Interview people, such as parents and grandparents, about vacations they have taken in the British Isles. Why did they choose to take their holiday in the British Isles? Record the answers on tape or video and edit your recording to make a documentary.

10 Using books, the Internet, and travel brochures, research one of the smaller islands of the British Isles, such as Herm. How big is the island? How many people live there? What is the landscape like? Does it have any special festivals and traditions?

11 Do an Internet search to find out about different island groups around the world. Do they have as many islands as the British Isles?

12 Find other places on the same latitude as the British Isles. Find out if the average temperatures are the same, or if they differ. Plot the results on a chart to compare the temperatures in the different places.

13 Using books and Web sites, find out about the beaches of the British Isles, and make a fact file. Make sections on tourism, wildlife, geology—or anything you find interesting.

14 Find out about where people came from when they emigrated to the British Isles in the 20th century. Why did people come to the British Isles? Make a world map and mark the countries people came from.

15 Imagine you are traveling across the British Isles. Write entries in an imaginary blog about your journey. What do you see? Who do you meet? Does anything funny happen to you? What do you learn about the British Isles?

16 Write a tourist leaflet describing a city in the British Isles. Remember to use exciting language to encourage people to visit.

17 Find out more about Hadrian's Wall from the English Heritage Web site. Then make a clay model of the wall.

18 Read some of Shakespeare's plays. You don't have to read the original versions—*Mr. William Shakespeare's Plays* by Marcia Williams is a great introduction; *Shakespeare Stories,* written by Leon Garfield and illustrated by Michael Foreman, tells the stories in an easy-to-understand way.

19 Do a Web search about landfill sites and their dangers. Make a poster about alternatives to landfill sites, including ways to reduce waste, such as recycling and reusing objects.

20 Find out more about Scottish Hogmanay traditions. Write a report as though you spent Hogmanay in Scotland and experienced it for yourself.

Glossary

arable land used for growing crops

beamed made from large pieces of timber. You can often see wooden beams both outside and inside very old houses

black pudding a type of sausage made from pork fat and pigs' blood

bubble and squeak leftover vegetables that are mixed together and fried

Celts Ancient peoples who lived in parts of the British Isles

clotted cream Very thick cream

dry dock a dock that can be drained of water and kept dry while work is being done on a boat

emigrated Having left one area or country to live in another

fortifications Thick walls or other ways to make a place safe from attack

freecycle An organization that helps people pass on things to other people, rather than throw them away

greenhouse gases Any of the gases in the atmosphere that contribute to global warming

Gulf Stream A warm ocean current that flows north from the Gulf of Mexico through to the Atlantic Ocean

hovercraft A boat driven by a propeller that has a cushion of air underneath. The cushion of air allows it to skim across the water

hydrofoil A boat that travels across the water very fast by skimming across the surface

landfill sites Where trash is dumped and then buried

latitude Distance from the equator (an imaginary circle around the middle of Earth, shown on most maps)

livestock Animals kept on a farm

loch Scottish word for a very deep lake

moorland An area of open land usually covered in coarse grass, bracken, heather, and moss

multicultural made up of people from many different cultural backgrounds

patties Small, flat cakes

Picts Ancient people of northern Britain

regional From a particular area or place

renewable energy "Green" energy, such as solar or wind power, that will never run out

smallholder A person who has a small farm and keeps animals and/or grows vegetables

solar panels Panels that trap and use the heat from sunlight

subtropical When the climate is hot in the summer and the winters are mild and rainy

temperate When the weather is never very hot nor very cold

thatched When the roof of a cottage or house is made of straw

wind farms Collections of wind turbines that generate electricity using the power of the wind

winter solstice A winter festival that happens on or about December 22nd in the Northern Hemisphere

Index

activities 28–30
animals 12
Appleby Fair 23
arable 18, 31
Arthur, King 21
Avalon 21

beaches 7, 12, 13, 27, 29
beamed 6, 31
Belfast 5, 15
black pudding 9, 31
Bonfire Night 22
Brighton 12, 13
bubble and squeak 9, 31

Caernarfon Castle 6
capital cities 5, 14–15
Cardiff 5, 14, 15
Celts 16, 20, 31
Channel Tunnel 11, 28
cities 5, 6, 14–15
climate 5, 7, 24–25
clotted cream 9, 31
coast 12–13, 30
conservation 26–27
currency 5

dry dock 15, 31
Dublin 5, 15
Dunstanburgh Castle 17

Edinburgh 5, 15
Edinburgh Festival 15
emigrated 7, 30, 31
environment 26–27

farming 18–19
Farne Islands 13
Fawkes, Guy 22
ferries 10
festivals 22–23
Fire Ceremonies 23
fish and chips 9
food 8–9, 19, 28, 29
fortifications 31
freecycle 27, 31
fruit 19

George IV, King 13
Giant's Causeway 20
Glastonbury Tor 21
Globe Theater, London 17
Gower Peninsula 13
greenhouse gases 27, 31
Gulf Stream 7, 13, 25, 31
Gunpowder Plot 22

Hadrian's Wall 16–17, 30
haggis 8
Herm 13, 29
hills 7
history 6, 16–17
Hogmanay 23, 30
holidays 22–23
hovercraft 10, 31
hydrofoil 10, 31

Ireland 8, 15
islands 5, 7, 29
Isle of Man 20

landfill sites 27, 30, 31
landscapes 7

languages 5
latitude 25, 29, 31
laver bread 8
Lewes 22
life expectancy 5
livestock 18, 31
location 5
Loch Ness monster 21
lochs 21, 31
London 5, 6, 11, 14, 17

maps 4, 28
moorland 7, 31
mountains 5
multicultural 7, 31
myths and legends 20–21

Ness, Loch 21

organic food 19
Orkney Islands 7

patties 8, 31
Picts 16, 31
piers 12
population 5
puffins 13

recycling 27, 30
regional 10, 31
religions 5
renewable energy 26, 29, 31
riverboats 11
rivers 5

St. Michael's Mount 20
Scotland 8, 12, 15, 21, 23, 25

seasons 24
Shakespeare, William 17
sheep 18
smallholders 19, 31
Snowdon Mountain Railw
   10, 11
solar panels 26, 31
Stratford-upon-Avon 17
subtropical 7, 31
surfing 13

temperate 5, 24, 31
Thames, River 6, 11
thatched 6, 31
Titanic 15
tourism 27, 28, 30
Tower Bridge 6
Tower of London 11
trains 11
transport 10–11

underground railways 10

Vikings 17
Vindolanda 17

Wales 8, 13, 15, 18
Wildlife Trusts 27
wind farms 26, 31
winter solstice 23, 31
woodland 7

York 17